College Journey 101

A Reference Manual for Freshmen

A.J. SHERMAN

Copyright © 2019 A.J. Sherman
All rights reserved
First Edition

PAGE PUBLISHING, INC.
New York, NY

First originally published by Page Publishing, Inc. 2019

This reference manual is intended to serve as a guide that helps prepare you for college success without the fear of starting college. It is for anyone who has been out of school for years and also someone who just want to keep up with the current college lifestyle.

ISBN 978-1-68456-549-8 (Paperback)
ISBN 978-1-68456-550-4 (Digital)

Printed in the United States of America

What doesn't kill you will make you stronger.

—Friedrich Nietzsche, philosopher

This manual was written because of my daughter, who inspired me to present the basic principles of college lifestyles and preparation for the journey of success.

CONTENTS

INTRODUCTION

As an African American citizen, "teacher," and parent, anyone like myself who wants to further their education should not have to struggle to obtain the information that's required to start. This book serves as a guide for beginners and freshmen who are on the path to their college journey. *College Journey 101* will hopefully make your transition to college exciting and a little smoother. This is for all of YOU who said can't do it. For all of YOU who said you don't know where to begin. Well, YOU can, and YOU should. Begin your college journey. *Good luck.*

CHAPTER 1

College Preparatory

You remember when your parents and grandparents all told you to keep up your grades? How you must work hard and play later. You remember that famous speech that was always said, "Don't go outside until you finish your homework." All the studying for test and projects that must be completed within a week. All the money spent for supplies and poster boards, calculators, composition notebooks, and special supplies, just to name a few. Also, a big part of college preparatory is being involved in your community. Become active, make a statement. Join a club or debate team. It will make a difference during your senior year. People will began to recognize your talents and potentials.

Testing

All the work you must prepare for chapter test, lectures, and quizzes prepare you for college. Each school testing site from the region prepares you to take the college SATs and ACT test. At these sites, you spend all day testing. You must be at the site approximately 7:00 a.m. to 3:00 p.m. or maybe let go sooner, depending on the location you are assigned to.

Deciding On A Major

After all the hard work and studying, you must choose a major and a minor. What do you have an interest in? What are your goals? What is your decision? Need help choosing a major? Why is choosing a major so important? How to choose a major that is right for you. You must decide on going to school full or part time. Are you willing to live on campus or stay at your parent's home and commute to and from school each day? Are you willing to drive in traffic, run across the campus field, stand in lines or get up, go outside your dorm room two-doors down? Or get dressed and in ten minutes be seated in class? How will college be paid for?

You must apply online to the colleges of your choice, then retrieve your scores from your high school or board of education. After those schools that you've chosen accepts you based on your scores, those scores and paperwork must be submitted. A FASFA form must also be submitted in a timely fashion. This FASFA form is usually due in January. You will receive the SAR if there are any issues with the FASFA form. The testing that takes place at these sites usually is given 7 times a year. When you apply early to schools you hear back in late March or early April. You are giving an opportunity to retake the test if your scores are not to your liking or are fairly low. You want to score the best scores possible because the higher the scores, the better your chances you have at getting into the school of your choice.

Also, another advantage of having high scores is that institutions will often give you a "full-ride scholarship." Another form of financial aid that is available is the Pell Grant and lastly is the student government loans. You can also apply for a private loan such as Sallie Mae, a discover card loan or pay out of pocket.

CHAPTER 2

Applying to a College

When applying to different colleges make certain you choose at least six different ones. You can apply online at the school's website or fill out a paper application. Once you submit your application online, you will need to download, print it, send the official document(s), and pay your application fee. If you have questions, then contact the college for help by e-mail at undergrad admissions or by phone. As a freshmen or transfer applicants, you must meet certain requirements. The applicant must fill in his/her demographics and personal information. Also, gender, date of birth, social security number, and such.

The qualifications to the application process are granted to all applicants who meet the college's admissions standards. These minimum standards are a GPA of 3.0 or better and a high SAT score. Although everyone has a deadline for the process, most requirements are time sensitive. During this application process, you must explore a major and an area of concentration. For first-time students, those who are graduating high school seniors and earned a high school diploma are required to submit their SAT/ACT scores and most recommendations from their counselors. To be considered for admissions, an application and all required documents must be submitted usually around February and November.

Tests should be taken in the spring for high school juniors and in the fall for high school senior year. If you need additional forms, they can be downloaded on the college website. While open house for most colleges/universities advertise what they offer, this is a good opportunity for you and your parent(s) or loved one to take advantage and see what is being offered. Learn about the academic programs, research opportunities, support services, student life, and financial aid. You will learn valuable information on the admission process and scholarship programs too.

The big moment has come when you are accepted to the college/university of your choice. Now you have received your acceptance letter of congratulations. This letter will come from the admissions office. It should state your student ID number and password, which all colleges use to communicate with the admitted student. All communications to you will come from the universities website that you will now have to login by your given e-mail address. The next step will be to confirm your acceptance by paying a fee usually about eighty to one hundred dollars, which is nonrefundable and returning a response card back with it. Another option is also calling student accounts.

In the year 2017, things have changed dramatically for the better. You must register for the (NSO) now that most colleges/universities have started. This is to introduce all they have to offer, take you on a school tour, provide you with a meal, hand out goods such as useful tools for class, backpacks, charges, school caps with the logos on them, and T-shirts.

All To Help Get You In The School Spirit

Also, some campuses offer one to three days stay on campus to help you better adjust to the housing arrangements. Forms are filled out, talks with several departments, music is played, and a host of other activities go on to help you decide is college life for you. If you decide to live on campus there, a housing application is provided by resident life that needs to be completed right away. When you come to the NSO, you must bring the required medical history/immunization record forms with you to the wellness center. These forms are a must have in order to register for classes or take the placement exams such as the ACCUPLACER test.

If you plan on living on campus, you are required to select a meal plan. Some are the regular or standard plans that range from seven days to nineteen-day meals. Some are very costly, but you will then learn how to adjust and make it work. This tool will teach you how to save and not waste money, whether it's yours or someone else hard earned money. As you attend the NSO, you should be given your student ID, meet the advisors, register for your classes, and pay your bill. Each university/college vary whether they have NSO or not and how each operates differently.

CHAPTER 3

College Campus Visits

It's a very exciting time in your life when you have just finished high school, or you have transferred from another college or university. You want to visit the college of your choice. All universities welcome newcomers and the like. First things first, you must call the campus and/or e-mail them to schedule a visit. One of the best ways to get to know college life is to visit the campus for the day. You may even be able to request to *shadow* a friend or student representative. Once you set up that visit, there is a lead person who will give a guided tour around the college campus for the day.

They will schedule you on a particular day and time—a time not to interfere with the students' schooling but as a way that will help you, the prospective freshmen. Also, you will be asked how many people will be accompanying you when you attend the tour, usually up to five people, and their names must also be listed. This tour will help you make a wise decision about attending that particular institution. You get most of your experience of the campus life through academics, athletic programs, and student organizations—fraternities and sororities.

During this guided tour, you will also discover the involvement of activities and programs, housing, and know the best forms of transportation to and from the campus. All kinds of pamphlets and brochures will be given out as well. There will also be maps to help familiarize you with how to get around the campus and the location of each department. As an added bonus, you get to meet your tour guide(s) and the other important people you will need to rely on for years to come.

While visiting, there is a visitors' parking area, and you must get a parking pass to place in your vehicle, that's if you're driving, of course. The last thing to do for parking is to provide your credentials, (driver's license or MD ID) and then sign in. As part of the tour, you will be told where the restrooms, snack machines, and eating areas are when you are given a break. An exciting part of college visits is seeing some great performances from the marching bands and step shows from the college fraternities or sororities. One of the most important parts of the guided tour is weighing your options. Know whether you belong to that institution or feel like you belong. Make sure you feel comfortable about your surroundings because this may be the very place you have to or want to spend your four years living and attending school. If this is what you want or where you want to be, talk to an advisor and an admissions officer then submit an application to start the entry process. *Follow your heart, not your friends.*

CHAPTER 4

Shopping for College and Dorms

Part 1: Shopping For Your Dorm

You know that school is about to start. You are excited and can't wait to shop for new stuff. These are the things that you need for your dorm room to make you feel comfortable and feel somewhat right at home. Also, the things to make you feel good.

You prepare by printing out a college dorm checklist/registry of some of the all-time favorite back-to-school headquarters like Walmart, Target, and Bed Bath & Beyond.

After getting your registry, you decide which store has better prices by comparison shopping. Next, you set a budget/limit for which you want to spend. You want to have all the necessary essentials, right? It's your freshmen year and what better way to start the new school off right. Besides, you don't want to start off having to ask your roomy or others for things you should have come with in the first place. One of the important parts about college dorm room shopping is to check with the colleges' resident hall policy on bringing in certain items. This policy states what you can or cannot bring in the dorms.

Another factor to figure in is how big something is or how many of something to bring in. After all, you must consider that you're not alone, and the rooms are usually shared by two of you. If you requested a single-dorm room, that's different, but most of the time, this request can only be done at most universities/colleges by juniors and seniors.

When making big purchases such as the microfridge combo, you have options to rent or split the bill with your roommate. Another thing about the microfridge combo is that it must be approved through resident living on campus. All approvals for certain items in the rooms will have to pass room inspection. Hopefully, while living on campus, you get someone who is compatible with you—someone who doesn't mind splitting the bill with you. The *disclaimer* about this roommate is that you may have the roommate from hell. They may also be someone who listens to loud music, someone who steals from you.

Another part of college shopping is bargain shopping and getting good deals any and everywhere you can. You may want to wait for back-to-school week that typically starts on the thirteenth or the third week in August. When getting the bedding, be sure to get the twin XL (extra-large) or dorm-size sheets.

Here is a list of items you may need to dress up your dorm room: sheets, twin XL, throw blanket, picture frames for your wall art, don't forget the magnetic strips, microfridge combo, lamps or wall lights, ironing board, iron and surge protectors.

Personals

1. towels and rags, two shower shoes
2. deodorant, toothpaste/brushes
3. laundry detergent, Lysol spray
4. first aid kit, waste basket
5. bars of soap/bodywash

Food and Utensils

1. cereal, bowls
2. noodle soup, beverages, cups
3. breakfast sandwiches, plates

4.   tuna kits
5.   popcorn, chips, crackers, fruit cups

Part 2: Shopping For Clothing

This is the other very important part of shopping for college. Although college is nothing like high school, you still have to look neat and clean, not so much for a lot of fashion but for the simple fact that you can basically wear what you want. No more uniforms. When shopping for these clothes, you must look unique. You must have what no one else has. You are no longer told what to wear as far as clothes go.

One important tradition that happens on some college campuses is you might see most freshmen wear the school sweatshirts with their logos on them. You want to represent for your institution on campus. You have that confidence that you now belong, and this further validates this. Your appearance helps further your confidence and allow you to feel comfortable and perform satisfactory or above-average level. Here is a list of items you may need: an umbrella, coat/jacket, flat, tennis, heels, pants, jeans, dress/skirts, glasses, watch, and cell phone.

School supplies

Writing equipment: pens, pencils, book light/lamp, laptop/ computer, book bag, dry erase board, printer.

CHAPTER 5

Move-In Day

This is one of the biggest days of your life. One of the days you have been waiting for. As part of the college process, you have the choice of staying or not staying on someone's college/university campus. This is what new students or freshmen call getting the college experience. As part of the last college process, each student will be given a student ID, username, and school e-mail address. This e-mail address and ID will help provide access to most of your college functions and privileges. You will need this information when looking at your schedules, financial aid, policies and procedures, dorm rules, school calendars, and other events. You will receive a scheduled move-in date according to your dorm room number, building, and floor.

Note: Some institutions may proceed by last name, but they all vary accordingly. This and other pertinent information is sent via e-mail or text message. One of the worst parts of this process is packing your belongings that need to be moved in. To help organize your precious items, you will need boxes. You can either purchase these boxes or get them from your local supermarket or convenient stores. You should organize each box by labeling and writing on each as personals, shoes, clothing, dorm items, school supplies, and food.

Depending on the college/university you attend, each move-in date has a specific time frame to help better organize the flow of traffic. Different activities take place on these move-in dates. You may have a live band or music, food stands, or dessert stands available.

Also, there will be ticket booths for games and prizes. There's always the unexpected. You may have bought too much to carry, so now you need something to carry all your items from the car to your dorm room. You can request to get a cart or dolly to load all your items at one time and take to your room.

Some college campuses require that you issue them a state ID or student ID. You will need this to check-in on check-in day. Next, you can obtain your dorm key and room inventory form. On this form, you must check off what is broken and list the needed repairs. When this is completed, you must turn it in to the dorm attendee(s).

Now that you have finished the following, you can move right in. One of the advantages of sticking to the time frame that is allotted for each student is getting to campus early. When you get to the campus early, you have first preferences when it comes to the room choices, beds, and which side of the room you want. Other options are which closet or desk is better that will accommodate your belongings. All the boxes and extras you carry along may seem like a lot, but if you pack your things right and organize, label the boxes and arrive on time, it will all be worth it.

At this point, you must be excited but overwhelmed. You may see some of your friends, maybe family members who attend the same university. You may want to unpack, socialize, eat, who knows. This is all part of the anxiety you are feeling from this moment. You may even have separation anxiety from your loved one(s). This is the first time in your life you will be apart from your mom, dad, or kids. It is now time to part and say goodbye. You are about to start your journey to college. Your mom or dad, kids have told you to keep in touch at least once a week. You may cry happy tears, but you will do just fine. Believe me, those of us who have once attended a university at some point in our lives have done so as well. We could not wait until the day we started and when it ended. In the words of the late great Michael Jackson, "You are not alone."

CHAPTER 6

The Start of College

The First Day

The first day of school can be exciting but overwhelming. You don't know what to expect. How should you come prepared? You are very nervous. What materials should you use in class for that day? Overall, the first day of class you can expect your instructor(s) or professor to review the syllabus, take attendance, explain what to expect from the course, the materials that will be covered, projects, test, home assignments when they all are due, the type of textbooks, and the chapters they will cover.

Tip no. 1: The first day is very important, so get your rest, be attentive, and be on time.

Tip no. 2: Take good notes.

Tip no. 3: Go to class.

Tip no. 4: Study for the test and try not to cram.

Tip no. 5: Whenever there are extra points given out, do the work. They help at the end of the semester and can boost low grades when needed.

College is not like high school. The syllabus is given out the first day, and most of the time, the work begins that day. The instructor will tell you immediately what materials are needed. Don't be surprised you may even receive homework the very first day. This is often a good time to find out what projects or big assignments may be due, so you can get a head start on them.

Also, you can expect the first day there is a crowd of people rushing all to the same location or building that you are. You are new so you may be a little late to class, so set your phone alarm to wake you. All the surrounding noises of shuffling bags and shouting makes your heart start pounding with exhaustion, excitement, and nervousness. You finally make it to class on time. You're not alone. You think you are though. Finally, you meet your classmates, and you feel a little at ease. Whoa…I know right. This class is over now.

Your next class starts in one hour. That gives you enough time to relax and grab something to eat. You socialize with your classmates and homegirls. You try to remember all that was said in class today. Did you copy what was important? It's not easy, but you did it. This is your last class, and it has ended. A life's lesson: In college, it's not important on how you look as long as you come to class clean and show up on time. Nevertheless, when you were in high school, it was based strictly on fashion.

CHAPTER 7

Are You Ready?

Are you really ready for college? College is like no other journey. We all know that college is completely different from high school, but once you've experienced the aspects of freedom, it may surprise you.

Independence

You may have lived at home with a parent who told you to come in at a certain time every night, or one who told you when to go to bed and when to eat, but now things have changed. Your parents are still a part of your life, but believe me, you will still need them more than ever for advice and some. However, the final decision on when to go to bed, get up for class, what to eat is yours and yours alone. This wonderful opportunity you so badly wanted is also frightening. No one will be there telling you what to wear to class, how to totally dress. No more really strict curfews.

In high school, you could count on your parents to support you, and I'm sure they'll help out, and you count on them from time to time, but now just not on a daily basis the way they were used to doing. The good thing about independence is growing up. And while growing up, you will make mistakes, but that's all apart of growth. You make a mistake, learn from it, then keep it from happening again or know what to do the next time it happens. Certain situations may happen that may make you rethink or organize your priorities.

For example, someone in your dorm may be having a party or end-of-the-year celebration. The celebration is, of course, on a school night, the day before a big test. You decide you will go and stay only for an hour, but you are having more fun than you've had all year. Your girlfriends have just arrived at the party. Although it started at 9:30 p.m., they show up at 10:30 p.m. What will you do? The big test is at 8:00 a.m. You still have to study, find something to wear for the next day and shower, not to mention you live off campus. Decisions, decisions. You start out with good intentions to do well, but things fall apart quickly. It's all a part of independence, and you will figure it out eventually.

Budgeting

It can be scary out there when you are in college and have to now budget what little monies you get. It can be work study monies you earn, an allowance your parents give you each week or month to get what small items and food you need. Monies you make doing hair or makeup, totaling about forty to sixty dollars a week. Living at college can also be a challenge with wanting to attend all the social gatherings held on and off campus. It can become very costly, so you choose which to attend and not to attend. If you want to keep the cost down, you will take heed to this.

Decision-Making

You obviously have made the decision to go to college, so the goal is to get a college degree, make something of yourself. But what? You will change your mind a hundred times or more, but the choice is yours. What will you major in? If you major in business, there will be so many options and paths to go to get there. The good but terrifying thing about college is that you may make pit stops along the way, go down many hills, and go around corners. You may speed up and slow down and then stop to take a break, but it's your decision to make, and your choice to decide which path you want to travel on your journey.

Work Ethics

You have come this far to succeed and achieve all your accomplishments from working hard thus far, but it's not over yet. College is completely different from high school—in that, the workload is much less, but the work will count for much more because each assignment will be worth more points. High school differs from college because in high school, you had what we like to call busywork, and you really weren't learning. But now every test, quiz, and class assignment counts for something.

Now that you're in college, you should develop better study habits, take better class notes, and develop time management skills. You will have more time to work on all of them, though starting early is the way to achieve success. The positive aspect of attending college and building good work ethics is that you get to make up your own class schedules. Unlike in high school, your classes, days, and the time were chosen for you for the most part. You are free to choose what class schedule you want. You can freely take a 12:00 p.m. class or 2:00 p.m. class if you want, Mondays to Fridays or Tuesdays to Thursday. That's what's good about college independence.

Starting and Finishing College

For many college students, there is no clear direction to finishing college and graduating. For most college students, they take more classes than needed and classes that don't count toward their graduation credits, if they graduate at all. For most, the first year freshmen the workload is not taking seriously. Freshmen are all about partying, and much is taking for granted. Most first-year students switch between full-time and part-time study, take time off from school to either work or visit family, and sometimes transfer to other four or two-year institutions. The thought of paying for college, on-campus living, food, books, transportation, and other expenses is an important factor when considering the trade-off of trying to obtain a four-year degree that is difficult to bear. However, college is easy to get in to; staying and finishing is hard but worth the effort.

Travel Expenses

Are you going to drive your own vehicle, or use public transportation? Driving your own vehicle has its pros and cons. Pros of driving your own vehicle are getting to class and activities on time, being able to come and go when you want, not having to travel in the rain or snow. Cons: paying for high-priced gas, paying for parking passes, looking for a place to park when it's crowded and when you're in a hurry.

Pros of using the public transportation is getting the student advantage discount card (SA). It is blue and white. This card will entitle students who ride the MARC train, light rail, subway, etc. to get a lower fare while using the services needed.

A student such as yourself can sign up online under MVA student services. You must fill the form out and mail it back into card enrollment services. The cost of this discount card is about $22.50 for one year, $32.50 for two years, and so on. This card expires exactly one year from the date of purchase. Don't mistake this card for the MARC train pass; this is different. It is used in conjunction with the MARC train pass. The MARC train pass can be purchased online at mta.maryland.gov and studentadvantage.com, and you will receive it within seven to ten business days or at any of the MARC train kiosk machines.

The MARC pass can cost up to $160 monthly without the student discount and $6.00 daily each way. With the student discount pass, a weekly pass can cost $38.50, monthly it would cost you $137.50. There are several locations near you. Martins Airport,

Baltimore Penn Line, Camden Line, Bowie and Brunswick Line. Each student is issued a member number that must be used with your college student identification card. However, until you receive your student advantage card, you can go to the MARC booths/stations and provide the station operator with your member number.

This member number consists of sixteen digits. In order to get the discounts, you must renew your application each year. The cons of using public transportation are having to be on time or on schedule with the train stations, being around so many weird people you know nothing about, and being around different cultures and attitudes. Also, the loud noises, shoving and pushing of people scurrying throughout the lines.

CHAPTER 8

Knowing and Finding Yourself

College life is hard enough, but knowing and finding out who you are can be an optimistic task. Do you really know who you are? Who you want to be, what you want to become? Well, you're not alone in this matter. It takes time to find yourself, but first, you have to stop searching. Love yourself for who you are, accept yourself, let yourself live, be happy with yourself and your shortcomings. Focus on you, put yourself first, travel, join a group, have faith in yourself, and try new things. Life is not what others want for you but what you want for yourself. It doesn't happen overnight, but when it does, you **will** know it.

The journey is real, but the final destination is extraordinary. Some things to consider while finding yourself is chasing your dreams, focusing on motivation, academic readiness, going from passive to active learning, support, and long-term opportunities. We are used to being accepted by our peers, fitting in groups, wanting for others to like us for what they see but not for who we truly are. We try to be someone we're not. There is more risk to being who we really are, so we live that lifestyle. We fall short on living the life we want trying to please those around us. We are lost in the world because we don't know ourselves.

If we lived our own lives, we would be comfortable without the fear of limitations, explanations, and participation in society. Knowing and finding yourself prohibits uncertainty. We live our lives with created daily routines. We go to school or work, come home, spend time with our loved ones. We read the paper or spend time doing school work, playing with kids, eating dinner, showering, and preparing for the next day. It's so scary because our routine is so predictable anyone who knows us can tell us what will happen next. We are afraid to step "outside the box."

Then there are some of us who become bored with this. These type of people are daredevils and risk takers. These type of people will try anything. Some of us lose ourselves in life and the people we associate ourselves around. You may be that person who will take long walks and not know where you will end up. We all make mistakes in life, and making mistakes is not necessarily a bad decision all the time. When you fail, it prepares you for greatness. We're all a diamond in the rough. All that means is that we can all become someone great, make something of ourselves. We just have to work hard at it, use our God-given talents.

Don't let someone tell you you're not capable of succeeding in life. Those that are lost in life don't always take the direct path to success. But not all those who wander are lost; they eventually find their way. These are some of the success stories today:

Ray Kroc, McDonald's founder, it took fifty-two years to become successful. J.K. Rowling, *Harry Potter* author, it took thirty-one years for success to happen.

Knowing and finding yourself is not at all bad. You get to discover the new you, the better you, the bad you, the stubborn you. Most of all, you accept it; the people around you deal with it. It's wonderful experiencing the inner you. Something you should know, if there's something in your heart, it will get you hooked.

Show me how to love, show me how to surrender my heart, show me how I can get my emotions involved, teach me. Quit breaking my heart, don't deny the truth. I know your heart is in the right place. Don't let me down.

Best of all, you should be fine with what you do, who you are, and how you look. If you want to be different, meaning you dress comfortable, colorful, and crazy, that's your business. Uncry those tears, say you love yourself, and move on. Be you, do you, and do it well. You may change your mind off and on so many times about living on a university campus and whether to go to college at all. Some undergraduates who have just finished high school may decide to go to college their first year, then may decide after that first year it is not what they want to do, so they decide to make some fast cash instead. This is all a part of growing up or the grown-up process, but it is your choice to decide.

Remember, college is not for everyone, and everyone is not college material.

CHAPTER 9

What It's Like to Live on Campus?

Living on campus is different from where you come from. The shared experience is different than what you're used to. Here's a chance to make it on your own if you focus on your goals. Just remember you've been told. What it's like to live on campus? It's the question that every college student must ask himself. Should you live on campus or off campus? Both questions have its advantages and disadvantages, so it is very important that you make a wise choice before making your final decision. To help you choose between the two, here are some pros and con of living on and off campus.

Pros: One of the perks is living away from home, living with new friends, having your freedom to be independence. Are you the type to keep to yourself, or are you sociable? You also get to experience being close to the university and not having to travel far to classes. But how do you know if living on campus is for you? Do you like to study alone? Are you a "worker bee?"

If your choice is to live on campus, then here are some of the benefits: you get what is called "the college experience," you get to further enhance your growth and independence. Also, when college events take place, you are there as soon as it happens. Besides, those that mature faster it is every girl and guys dream to someday have his/her own apartment or home away from home. You may have a roommate to start out with, but by the time you finish college, you will have made a lifelong friend. Besides, being on your own, you can shop for food and other items the way you like. You get to eat what you like, how you like it.

The Cons: Living on campus and sharing dorm rooms with a total stranger, sharing a bathroom with more than one person, and all the noise and disturbances that distract you from studying and passing that big exam you must take. Lastly, one that is of value to some who is family oriented is not having a home-cooked meal each night. Also, not having leftovers in the refrigerator when you want it.

Make a choice and stick with it. It is one that you will have to decide and have to live with. With all the excitement of finishing your twelve years of high school and after listening to your siblings who have attended a college or university, you now want to see what it's like for yourself.

When you come home on spring break, winter break, Christmas break, and others alike, your family members crowd you of conversation. The first thing that is asked of you when you arrive home after being gone for so long is "How do you enjoy living on campus and being away from home?" What it's like to live on campus? One thing for sure, two things for certain, it's not a walk in the park. Living on campus is like living in your own little studio apartment but with a lived-in border. Another similarity of living on campus is the tight living conditions and lack of space. The only thing is that neither of you are not paying rent; you're both paying tuition for housing.

And in case you didn't catch on…yes, tuition is more expensive. Also, some college campuses do have curfews, just like at home. Living on campus and sharing rooms with a total stranger you don't know can be an "eye-opener." Your roommate could be eating your food and saving his, sleeping in your bed, turning on your microwave and heating up food without your permission. You also don't know if your roomy is nosing through your belongings or using your deodorant and other hygiene products.

This is the magical question you have to ask yourself. Is this what I really want to do? How do you become involved in the campus activities around you? There are a host of sports like volleyball, tennis, track, table hockey, and swimming pools. If you like hanging around the campus and want to relax, you can go to the library or music halls.

There are a variety of cafés and restaurants if you want to try different foods out when you're hungry. It is said that those who live on campus excel a little better than those not living on campus because of the close proximity of the classes. Aside from all the "hype" that is said around campuses these days, you do have your slow or boring days where there is absolutely nothing to do.

Take heed. This is the best time to catch up on sleep, projects, home assignments, and the cleaning up of your side of the room and reorganizing of small things. Part of living on a college campus is budgeting and maintaining some order of how you spend your money. You need to understand that the struggle is real. First thing you should do if you haven't already done so is to set up a bank account. If you are fortunate to get a part-time job and one that is on campus, save, save, save your money.

You need to understand that you should only spend what is necessary for classes or products you may need. I know this is hard to do when you have all the activities staring you in the face. Remember, another option may be to get what is called a "side hustle" going. If you have any experiences at doing hair, makeup, barbering, or even trading a product for service. One that is legal, of course.

There are all types of services that can be traded such as the typing of term papers for money. What it's like to live on campus you ask again? The key to living on campus is surviving, independency, socializing, and being responsible. So if this is what you want to do, if this is your choice, go for it, make the best of it, and see it through.

Main point is to concentrate and avoid the distractions at all cost. It's hard, but you can do it. It takes guts and willpower. You will thank yourself for it later. Another very important part of living on campus is having parental support. Your family should positively encourage you to do well, provide you with moral support and monetary support if they are capable of doing so. Live the college dream, be the best at whatever you are trying to excel in. If you fail to live, you live to fail.

CHAPTER 10

Undergrad to Grad

When you are an undergraduate, you take more classes, the classes are larger, and it is easy to move from class to class. It is also easier to move from school to school. Postundergraduate studies you earn an associate's degree and a bachelor's degree. Graduate studies or grads as they are normally called, the classes are much smaller in size and require specialized classes such as philosophy. When you are a grad, you have fewer classes, and it is more difficult to move around from school to school. Most grads earn a master's degree and doctoral degree. The famous doctor named Dr. Ben Carson once worked in Baltimore's well-known hospital called John's Hopkins Hospital. He who separated the Siamese twins at birth graduated and was determined to set high standards for himself.

At the graduate level, the professors teach on a one-on-one basis. Also, you as the student are expected to perform at your own pace instead of project-based and class assignments are mostly discussions and debates instead of lectures and discussions. The average graduate is approximately thirty years or older. At the graduate level, the content is specific about career focus and mind-building sets, which helps to make the individual well-rounded. Unlike undergraduate studies, there is not a broad range of content to create as a well-rounded person.

In undergraduate work, the focus is on learning information; it's about memorization and understanding concepts. Graduate school is very different. When you reach the graduate level of courses, the focus switches from learning the information to applying it. At the undergraduate level, professors or lecturers give you more structured projects, detailed outlines, outlined notes and detailed directions and time lines to complete assignments, so you know what's expected of you.

Graduate level of studies, you'll have less structure and plenty of freedom to do as you please; so learn to manage your time wisely. There will be more reading and researching to do and less writing than usual. Your mind-set is expected to be different. Your professors will hope for you to be a key contributor to class discussions. They will also talk to you and treat you like you are contributing to class discussions while learning and sharing your experiences at the same time. Be ready for the extra effort. The learning at this level is what some universities call the "360 learning." You will be networking with your peers but working with professors as well.

Remember, freedom equals responsibility without someone constantly reminding you of those deadlines. So you need to manage your deadlines and stay up on your reading so that you don't fall behind. This includes both large and small. Graduate work is not a piece of cake.

CHAPTER 11

Acronyms and Definitions

1. Take heed: take notice, be aware, forewarned.
2. The hype: all the noise, what's happening, activities going on.
3. College experience: the life of a freshman or transfer student; those living on campus.
4. Worker bee: someone who works very hard; students who are heavily involved in their studies.
5. Perks: goods given for a service or job
6. Eye-opener: something that gets your attention. Something that excites you or get you going.
7. Side hustle: extra cash flow. Money that is earned other than a government job; a (9 to 5).
8. Privileges: the right to do something special.
9. Compatible: equal to a person, place, or thing.
10. Outside the box: an unusual way of thinking, thinking more than the norm.
11. ACT/SAT: American College Testing; Scholastic Assessment Test (formerly aptitude test).
    FAFSA: Free Application for Federal Student Aid.
    NSO: New Student Orientation.
12. SAR: Student Aid Report
13. College journey: experiencing college life by living it, taking classes, and having set goals.

14. Shadow: to shadow someone is to see how that person lives on or off campus and follow their daily activities and take the same classes that he/she takes.
15. Full-ride scholarship: an academic scholarship that pays for all expenses, which includes tuition, housing, extra fees, and sometimes books.
16. Goals: ambitions, plan, effort, purpose, target.
17. Resources: a supply of money, technology, professors, or other assets that can be drawn on by a person or organization in order to function effectively.
18. Organization: an organized group of one or more persons to serve a particular purpose. They plan and arrange for the sake of a business or the society.
19. Responsibility: the act of having control of something or someone; the right to be independent of one's actions.
20. Disclaimer: Denial or repudiation.
21. GPA: Grade Point Average.
22. 360 Learning: A high level of learning. Effective student and teacher relationship. Provides work-ready students and quality teaching.

CHAPTER 12

Sample College/University Forms

UNIVERSAL
college APPLICATION

First-Year Admissions Application

This form is developed for, and is to be used by, the members of the Universal College Application. All members evaluate this form equally with all other forms accepted by the institution. Please type or print neatly.

College Name ______________________________

☐ Regular Decision I   ☐ Early Decision I
☐ Regular Decision II   ☐ Early Decision II
☐ Restrictive Early Action   ☐ Early Action

I am applying for the term beginning ______________________________

Possible Major ______________________________ Possible Career Plans ______________________________

PAYMENT INFORMATION

Are you planning to apply for a counselor approved fee waiver?   ☐ Yes   ☐ No   Are you applying for financial aid?   ☐ Yes   ☐ No

If you are applying for financial aid, when did/will you file the appropriate form(s) (FAFSA, CSS Profile, etc.)? ______________________________

PERSONAL INFORMATION

Please enter your name as it appears on your passport or other official documents.

Legal Name ______________________________ Date of Birth ______________________________
Last (Family)   First   Middle   Suffix (Jr., Sr., etc.)   (mm/dd/yyyy)

Legal Sex: ☐ Male   ☐ Female   Gender Identity (optional): ☐ Man   ☐ Woman   ☐ Self Identify ______________________________   Social Security Number (optional) ______________________________ Not Printed on PDF (###-##-####)

Preferred Name ______________________________ Previous Last Name(s), if any ______________________________

Email ______________________________ Marital Status ______________________________ (single, married, etc.)

PERMANENT ADDRESS

______________________________ ______________________________
Street Address   Apt. #

______________________________ ______________________________
City/Town   State/Province   Country   Zip/Postal Code

Phone ______________________________ Alternate Phone ______________________________
Begin with Area or Country Code   Begin with Area or Country Code

Please give your current address for all admission correspondence, if different from above.

CURRENT MAILING ADDRESS

______________________________ ______________________________
Street Address   Apt. #

______________________________ ______________________________
City/Town   State/Province   Country   Zip/Postal Code

Current Mailing Address Phone ______________________________ Current mailing address valid from ______________ to ______________
Begin with Area or Country Code   (mm/dd/yyyy)   (mm/dd/yyyy)

CITIZENSHIP

Place of Birth ______________________________
City/Town   State/Province   Country

☐ US Citizen   ☐ Dual US citizen; please specify other country of citizenship ______________________________

☐ US permanent resident visa; citizen of ______________________________ Alien registration number ______________________________

☐ Other Citizenship ______________________________
Visa

If you live in the United States, but are not a U.S. citizen, how many years have you lived in the country? ______________________________

If not English, language spoken in your home ______________________________ If not English, list your first language ______________________________

A.J. SHERMAN

ETHNICITY

Race/Ethnicity information is optional. Information you provide will not be used in a discriminatory manner.

Are you Hispanic or Latino? ☐ Yes ☐ No   (country of family's origin _______________________)

How would you describe your racial background? (select one or more of the following categories):

☐ Asian (country of family's origin _______________)   ☐ Native Hawaiian or Other Pacific Islander
☐ Black or African American   ☐ White
☐ American Indian or Alaska Native (enrolled _______________)
   Tribal affiliation _______________________

FAMILY INFORMATION

PARENT/GUARDIAN #1

☐ Parent ☐ Guardian _______________________
        Title   Last (Family)   First   Middle   Suffix

☐ Male ☐ Female   Living? ☐ Yes ☐ No (Date Deceased_______________)
        (mm/yyyy)

If different from yours
Address _______________________
     Street Address   Apt. #

____
City/Town   State/Province   Country   Zip / Postal Code

Phone _______________________   Email _______________________
  Begin with Area or Country Code

Profession _______________________   Position _______________________

Employer _______________________

College Attended (if any) _______________   Degree Earned _______________   Year _______

Graduate School Attended (if any) _______________   Highest Degree Earned _______________   Year _______

PARENT/GUARDIAN #2

☐ Parent ☐ Guardian _______________________
        Title   Last (Family)   First   Middle   Suffix

☐ Male ☐ Female   Living? ☐ Yes ☐ No (Date Deceased _______________)
        (mm/yyyy)

If different from yours
Address _______________________
     Street Address   Apt. #

____
City/Town   State/Province   Country   Zip / Postal Code

Phone _______________________   Email _______________________
  Begin with Area or Country Code

Profession _______________________   Position _______________________

Employer _______________________

College Attended (if any) _______________   Degree Earned _______________   Year _______

Graduate School Attended (if any) _______________   Highest Degree Earned _______________   Year _______

Your parents are _______________________   If divorced, list date _______________
    (married, divorced, etc.)   (mm/yyyy)

With whom do you reside? ☐ Both   ☐ Parent/Guardian#1   ☐ Parent/Guardian#2   ☐ Other (Explain) _______

List names, legal sex, and ages of your siblings, college (if any), degree(s), and dates of attendance.

Name	Legal Sex	Age	Institution	Degree(s)	Dates

ACADEMIC INFORMATION

School _______________________________________   CEEB Code _______________

Type of school: ☐ Public   ☐ Private   ☐ Correspondence   ☐ Charter   ☐ Parochial   ☐ Home School   ☐ Other/Education Provider

School Address ____
Number and Street

City/Town   State/Province   Country   Zip/Postal Code

Start Date _______________   Date of Graduation _______________
(mm/yyyy)   (mm/yyyy)

Counselor's Name _______________   Phone _______________
Begin with Area or Country Code

Counselor's Email _______________   Fax _______________
Begin with Area or Country Code

Are you currently enrolled in school?   ☐ Yes   ☐ No   Will/did you graduate from High School early?   ☐ Yes   ☐ No

Did you recieve a GED?   ☐ Yes   ☐ No   If so, list date: _______________   (Please send official scores from testing agency)
(mm/yyyy)

If your education has been interrupted, please detail your activities since last enrolled. Please attach your response to the end of the application.

CURRENT YEAR'S COURSES
Please list name, level (Honors, AP, IB, etc.) and credit value of your current year's courses.

Semester #1/Trimester #1	Semester #2/Trimester #2	Trimester #3

List all other high schools, colleges/universities (including summers), and academic programs you attended, beginning with ninth grade. You must submit transcripts from each school.

OTHER HIGH SCHOOLS

School Name	CEEB Code	Dates Attended	Location

COLLEGES/UNIVERSITIES

School Name	CEEB Code	Dates Attended	Location

FINANCIAL AID

Monthly Payments with Housing ______

Monthly Payments without Housing ______

HOUSING APPLICATION FOR CAMPUS HOUSING AT PARKVIEW TERRACE IN REDLANDS

Thank you for your interest in School Sponsored Housing! We look forward to having you join our community. In order to ensure your space within School-Sponsored Housing at **Parkview Terrace at 1601 Barton Road, Redlands, CA 92373,** you will need to:

1. Be enrolled as a student at The Art Institute of California—Inland Empire – for questions call the Admissions office at 909.915.2100.

2. Complete this application as thoroughly and honestly as possible.

3. Send your application and to The Art Institute of California—Inland Empire at the following address:

    The Art Institute of California—Inland Empire
Brian Rountree, Residential Life Coordinator
Attn: Student Services, Room 192
674 E. Brier Drive
San Bernardino, CA 92408

*Deposit may be paid by Cash or Credit/Debit card in amount of $150.00 to the Accounting Office (909.915.2100) located on the 2nd floor of the Main Building.

*Questions may be addressed by calling: **Brian Rountree,** Residential Life Coordinator, 909.915.2172 (office), or by email at brountree@aii.edu.

PLEASE WRITE LEGIBLY

Date: ____/____/_______

First Name: _______________   Middle Initial: ______   Last Name: : _______________

Student ID # __________   SS# ___ ___ ____   Sex: Male ___ Female___

Birthdate: ____/____/_____

Address: _______________________________

City ______________________   State ________   Zip Code __________

Country: _______________________

Phone # _______________   E-mail _____________________________________

Student Affairs

AI The Art Institute of California
A College of Argosy University
Inland Empire

45

Admissions Representative: _______________________________________

What quarter will you be moving into housing (please circle)?:
Fall   Winter   Spring   Summer

Academic Program: _______________________________

New Student: _______   Current Student: _______   Transfer Student: _______

Please provide information regarding any disciplinary matters you were involved in at any Art Institute or other post-secondary schools you have attended.

Have you ever been convicted of or pled guilty to a crime other than a summary traffic offense?
_______ Yes   _______ No

Do you have any documented disabilities or medical conditions of which housing staff should be made aware?
☐ Yes
☐ No

Signature: _______________________________________

Printed Name: _______________________________________

Today's Date: _______________________________________

Please complete the Roommate Preference Guide below.
In order to identify some of your attitudes about living with another person, answer the following questions honestly.   We encourage you to complete this questionnaire on your own, without input from friends and family.

Are you an early/morning or night person?
- ☐ Early/Morning
- ☐ Night

Describe your cleaning and housekeeping habits
- ☐ Cluttered
- ☐ Rarely clean
- ☐ Sometimes clean
- ☐ Usually clean
- ☐ Very clean

What are your study habits?
- ☐ Daily
- ☐ Weekly
- ☐ Last minute

What are your study preferences?
- ☐ I need a quiet place
- ☐ I can study with distractions

Please check the music styles you prefer: (select all that apply)
- ☐ Alternative
- ☐ Classic Rock/Rock
- ☐ Rap/ R&B
- ☐ Pop
- ☐ House
- ☐ Country
- ☐ Religious
- ☐ Classical
- ☐ Other ______________________________

My out-of-school activities include the following: (select all that apply)
- ☐ Work
- ☐ Sports/Recreation
- ☐ Reading/Watching TV/Movies
- ☐ Playing video games
- ☐ Going out of town
- ☐ School clubs/activities

Do you have a car?
- ☐ Yes
- ☐ No

What is your plan for transportation to and from school while living in school sponsored housing?

- ☐ Car
- ☐ Shuttle Service
- ☐ Public Transportation

Do you smoke?	Can you live with a smoker?
☐ Yes	☐ Yes
☐ No	☐ No

Select items that are important to you in matching with your roommate

- ☐ Age
- ☐ Study Habits
- ☐ Morning /Night Person
- ☐ Music Preferences
- ☐ Housekeeping Habits
- ☐ Major

I give my permission to release my name, phone number and email address to my roommate(s) once room assignments have been made.

- ☐ Yes
- ☐ No

Three words that describe my personality would be:

1.
2.
3.

Three words that describe my ideal roommate would be:

1.
2.
3.

Roommate Preference:
I would like to room with the following person: _______________________________________

Is there anything else that you think is important for The Art Institute of California- Inland Empire to know about your housing requests and needs?

Is there anything else that you think is important for your prospective roommate to know about your housing requests and needs (please attach additional sheets if necessary)?

AP/IB TEST SCORES

Please list any Advanced Placement or International Baccalaureate exams taken along with the test date and score.

Test Date	Subject	Score		Test Date	Subject	Score

STANDARDIZED TEST INFORMATION

List your test scores below. You must have the testing agency send official scores to each institution to which you are applying.

SAT Reasoning

Test Date	Verbal/ Critical Reading	Math	Writing		Test Date	Verbal/ Critical Reading	Math	Writing

SAT Subject

Test Date	Subject	Score		Test Date	Subject	Score

ACT

Test Date	English	Math	Reading	Science	Composite	Combination English/Writing Writing Subject Score

Test of English as a Foreign Language (TOEFL or other exam)

Test Date	Subject	Score		Test Date	Subject	Score

ACADEMIC DISTINCTIONS

Please list any academic or educational awards and honors you received in high school (e.g. National Merit, National Honor Society). Please attach your response to the end of the application.

EXTRACURRICULAR AND VOLUNTEER INFORMATION (including summer)

Please list any significant extracurricular or community activities and hobbies in which you have participated. Include specific accomplishments such as musical accolades, athletic distinctions, etc. (Please note: "PG" means Post Graduate)

Activity	Grade Level	Specific Accomplishments	Hours/ Week	Weeks/ Year	Will you participate in college?
__________	☐9 ☐10 ☐11 ☐12 ☐PG	__________	______	______	☐Yes ☐No ☐Unsure
__________	☐9 ☐10 ☐11 ☐12 ☐PG	__________	______	______	☐Yes ☐No ☐Unsure
__________	☐9 ☐10 ☐11 ☐12 ☐PG	__________	______	______	☐Yes ☐No ☐Unsure
__________	☐9 ☐10 ☐11 ☐12 ☐PG	__________	______	______	☐Yes ☐No ☐Unsure
__________	☐9 ☐10 ☐11 ☐12 ☐PG	__________	______	______	☐Yes ☐No ☐Unsure
__________	☐9 ☐10 ☐11 ☐12 ☐PG	__________	______	______	☐Yes ☐No ☐Unsure
__________	☐9 ☐10 ☐11 ☐12 ☐PG	__________	______	______	☐Yes ☐No ☐Unsure

EMPLOYMENT INFORMATION

List any work experience (including summer jobs) during the past three years.

Employer	Job Description	Dates of Employment	Hours per week
__________	__________	__________	__________
__________	__________	__________	__________
__________	__________	__________	__________
__________	__________	__________	__________
__________	__________	__________	__________

ACTIVITY DESCRIPTION

Tell us more about one of your extracurricular, volunteer, or employment activities (100 150 words). If you need more space, please attach your response to the end of the application.

PERSONAL STATEMENT

Please write an essay (650 words or fewer) that demonstrates your ability to develop and communicate your thoughts. Some ideas include: a person you admire; a life changing experience; or your viewpoint on a particular current event. Please attach your response to the end of your application.

MULTIMEDIA INFORMATION

Optional: You may provide your selected college(s) with a link to any online content you feel:
1. Tells the college more about yourself 2. Demonstrates a particular talent you possess 3. Highlights an activity in which you participated

Some ideas include linking to an online video you created, a portfolio (pictures or photographs), a musical composition, or a newspaper article.

http:// ____

Please briefly describe the contents of the link you provided.

ADDITIONAL INFORMATION

If you have additional information that was not specifically requested on the application or did not fit in the space provided, feel free to include it here. If you need more space, please attach your response to the end of the application.

DISCIPLINE INFORMATION

Have you ever been placed on probation, suspended, removed, dismissed or expelled from any school
or academic program since 9th grade?   ☐ Yes   ☐ No

Other than traffic offenses, have you ever been convicted of any misdemanor or felony?   ☐ Yes   ☐ No

If you answered yes to either question, please provide an explanation and the approximate dates of each incident.
Please attach your response to the end of the application.

AUTHORIZATION

Your signature below

1. authorizes all schools you attended to provide all requested records and allow review of your application for the admission process chosen on this application.

2. confirms all information in this application (including any supplemental information) is factually true and honestly presented and that you are the person submitting this application.

Signature of applicant ____________________________________   Date _________________________________

Graduate College
sample text
full standing admission letter from program
revised 11 October 2010

(Date)
(Applicant Name)
(Applicant Address)
(Applicant Address)

Dear *(Applicant Name)*:

I am pleased to inform you that your application for admission for *(term and year)* has been favorably reviewed *(by our Admissions Committee)*. We have recommended to the Graduate College that you are to be admitted on full graduate standing to the *(degree name)* program in *(program name)*.

The final decision on admission is made by the Graduate College. If they concur with our recommendation, and if all necessary documents have been received by the Office of Graduate Admissions, you will shortly receive notice of their decision, information concerning registration procedures and a url to *UIC Connect*, an informational website for newly admitted applicants. If you do not receive the official admit letter shortly, please contact me *(or other program contact)*. *(Term)* begins *(date)*.

If you have any questions concerning the admission or any aspect of the graduate program, please do not hesitate to contact *(advisor or other program contact name)* at *(address, email and/or telephone number)*.

On behalf of our faculty, I congratulate you on your promising academic record, and I hope you will be able to join our program. We are very happy that you have considered UIC for your graduate studies.

Sincerely,

(dgs name)
Director of Graduate Studies

c: *(advisor name)*, Advisor

Points to be Included in Full Standing Admit Letter
• *Recommendation* for admission was made to the Graduate College
• Term of admission
• Degree program admitted to (eg. Master of Science in ___________)
• Official admission letter will follow from the Office of Graduate Admissions (OAR) (assuming required credentials have arrived, etc.)
• Registration and *UIC Connect* information will follow from the Office of Graduate Admissions

A.J. SHERMAN

SAMPLE IMMUNIZATION RECORD

This is a SAMPLE immunization record form. If reproduced for use by a college or university health center, please insert your health center's contact information. This form should not be returned to ACHA. Please view the ACHA Guidelines: Recommendations for Prematriculation Immunizations (available at www.acha.org/Guidelines) for additional information.

PART I

Name ____   ____
First Name   Middle Name

____
Last Name

Address ____
Street   City   State   Zip

Date of Entry ____/________   Date of Birth ____/____/________   School ID# ____________________________
M   Y   M   D   Y

Status: Part-time ____   Full-time ____   Graduate ____   Undergraduate ____   Professional

PART II: TO BE COMPLETED AND SIGNED BY YOUR HEALTH CARE PROVIDER.

All information must be in English.

A. MMR (MEASLES, MUMPS, RUBELLA)

(Two doses required at least 28 days apart for students born after 1956 and all health care professional students.)

1. Dose 1 given at age 12 months or later ....#1 ____/____/________
M   D   Y

2. Dose 2 given at least 28 days after first dose ....,#2 ____/____/________
M   D   Y

B. MENINGOCOCCAL QUADRIVALENT

(A, C, Y, W-135) One or 2 doses for all college students; revaccinate every 5 years if increased risk continues.

1. Quadrivalent conjugate (preferred; administer simultaneously with Tdap if possible).

a. Dose #1 ____/____/________   b. Dose #2 ____/____/________
M   D   Y   M   D   Y

2. Quadrivalent polysaccharide (acceptable alternative if conjugate not available).

Date ____/____/________
M   D   Y

C. TETANUS, DIPHTHERIA, PERTUSSIS

1. Primary series completed?   Yes ____   No ____   Date of last dose in series: ____/____/________
M   D   Y

2. Date of most recent booster dose: ____/____/________   Type of booster: Td ______   Tdap ______
M   D   Y   *Tdap booster recommended for ages 11-64 unless contraindicated*

D. HEPATITIS B

(All college and health care professional students. Three doses of vaccine or two doses of adult vaccine in adolescents 11–15 years of age, or a positive hepatitis B surface antibody meets the requirement.)

1. Immunization (hepatitis B)

a. Dose #1 ____/____/________   b. Dose #2 ____/____/________   c. Dose #3 ____/____/________
M   D   Y   M   D   Y   M   D   Y

Adult formulation ____ Child formulation ____   Adult formulation ____ Child formulation ____   Adult formulation ____ Child formulation ____

2. Immunization (Combined hepatitis A and B vaccine)

a. Dose #1 ____/____/________   b. Dose #2 ____/____/________   c. Dose #3 ____/____/________
M   D   Y   M   D   Y   M   D   Y

3. Hepatitis B surface antibody   Date ____/____/________   Result: Reactive __________   Non-reactive __________
M   D   Y

(continues)

SAMPLE IMMUNIZATION RECORD (CONTD.)

E. INFLUENZA

Trivalent (IIV3) _____ Quadrivalent (IIV4) _____ Recombinant (RIV3) _____ Live attenuated influenza vaccine (LAIV) _____

Date of last dose: ___/___/_____
            M   D   Y

F. VARICELLA

(Birth in the U.S. before 1980, a history of chicken pox, a positive varicella antibody, or two doses of vaccine meets the requirement.)

1. History of Disease   Yes ___   No ___   or   Birth in U.S. before 1980   Yes ___   No ___

2. Varicella antibody   ___/___/_____   Result: Reactive _________   Non-reactive _________
                       M D   Y

3. Immunization

   a. Dose #1 ....#1 ___/___/_____
                                                                 M   D   Y

   b. Dose #2 given at least 12 weeks after first dose ages 1–12 years. ....#2 ___/___/_____
   and at least 4 weeks after first dose if age 13 years or older.   M   D   Y

G. HUMAN PAPILLOMAVIRUS VACCINE (HPV2/HPV4/HPV9)

(Three doses of vaccine for females and males 11–26 years of age at 0, 1–2, and 6 month intervals.)

Immunization (indicate which preparation, if known)   Quadrivalent (HPV4) _____   or   Bivalent (HPV2) _____   or 9-valent (HPV9) _____

a. Dose #1 ___/___/_____   b. Dose #2 ___/___/_____   c. Dose #3 ___/___/_____
       M   D   Y   M   D   Y   M   D   Y

H. HEPATITIS A

1. Immunization (hepatitis A)

    a. Dose #1 ___/___/_____   b. Dose #2 ___/___/_____
          M   D   Y   M   D   Y

2. Immunization (Combined hepatitis A and B vaccine)

    a. Dose #1 ___/___/_____   b. Dose #2 ___/___/_____   c. Dose #3 ___/___/_____
          M   D   Y   M   D   Y   M   D   Y

I. PNEUMOCOCCAL POLYSACCHARIDE VACCINE

PCV 13 _______   Date ___/___/_____   PPSV 23 _______   Date ___/___/_____
                  M   D   Y   M   D   Y

J. MENINGOCOCCAL SEROUGROUP B

(Two or three dose series; may be given to any college student or for outbreak control; may be given with quadrivalent meningococcal vaccine at different anatomic site. Must complete series with the same vaccine.)

1. MenB-RC (Bexsero)   __ routine   ____ outbreak –related

    a. Dose #1 ___/___/_____   b. Dose #2. ___/___/_____
            M   D   Y   M   D   Y

OR

1. MenB-FHbp (Trumenba)   __ routine   ___ outbreak-related

    a. Dose #1 ___/___/_____   b. Dose #2 ___/___/_____   c. Dose #3 ___/___/_____
            M   D   Y   M   D   Y   M   D   Y

I. POLIO

(Primary series, doses at least 28 days apart. Three primary series are acceptable. See ACIP website for details.)

1. OPV alone (oral Sabin three doses):   #1 ___/___/_____   #2 ___/___/_____   #3 ___/___/_____
                                   M   D   Y   M   D   Y   M   D   Y

2. IPV/OPV sequential: IPV #1 ___/___/_____   IPV #2 ___/___/_____   OPV #3 ___/___/_____   OPV #4 ___/___/_____
                      M   D   Y   M   D   Y   M   D   Y   M   D   Y

3. IPV alone (injected Salk four doses):   #1 ___/___/_____   #2 ___/___/_____   #3 ___/___/_____   #4 ___/___/_____
                                    M   D   Y   M   D   Y   M   D   Y   M   D

(continues)

SAMPLE IMMUNIZATION RECORD (CONTD.)

M. TUBERCULOSIS (TB) SCREENING/TESTING[1]

Please answer the following questions:

Have you ever had close contact with persons known or suspected to have active TB disease?   ☐ Yes   ☐ No

Were you born in one of the countries or territories listed below that have a high incidence of active TB disease?   ☐ Yes   ☐ No
(If yes, please CIRCLE the country, below)

Afghanistan	Congo	Iran (Islamic Republic of)	Namibia	Solomon Islands
Algeria	Côte d'Ivoire	Iraq	Nauru	Somalia South Africa
Angola	Democratic People's Republic	Kazakhstan	Nepal	South Sudan
Anguilla	of Korea	Kenya	Nicaragua	Sri Lanka
Argentina	Democratic Republic of the	Kiribati	Niger	Sudan
Armenia	Congo	Kuwait	Nigeria	Suriname
Azerbaijan	Djibouti	Kyrgyzstan	Northern Mariana Islands	Swaziland
Bangladesh	Dominican Republic	Lao People's Democratic	Pakistan	Tajikistan
Belarus	Ecuador	Republic	Palau	Thailand
Belize	El Salvador	Latvia	Panama	Timor-Leste
Benin	Equatorial Guinea	Lesotho	Papua New Guinea	Togo
Bhutan	Eritrea	Liberia	Paraguay	Trinidad and Tobago
Bolivia (Plurinational State	Estonia	Libya	Peru	Tunisia
of)	Ethiopia	Lithuania	Philippines	Turkmenistan
Bosnia and Herzegovina	Fiji	Madagascar	Poland	Tuvalu
Botswana	French Polynesia	Malawi	Portugal	Uganda
Brazil	Gabon	Malaysia	Qatar	Ukraine
Brunei Darussalam	Gambia	Maldives	Republic of Korea	United Republic of
Bulgaria	Georgia	Mali	Republic of Moldova	Tanzania
Burkina Faso	Ghana	Marshall Islands	Romania	Uruguay
Burundi	Greenland	Mauritania	Russian Federation	Uzbekistan
Cabo Verde	Guam	Mauritius	Rwanda	Vanuatu
Cambodia	Guatemala	Mexico	Saint Vincent and the	Venezuela (Bolivarian
Cameroon	Guinea	Micronesia (Federated States	Grenadines	Republic of)
Central African Republic	Guinea-Bissau	of)	Sao Tome and Principe	Viet Nam
Chad	Guyana	Mongolia	Senegal	Yemen
China	Haiti	Montenegro	Serbia	Zambia
China, Hong Kong SAR	Honduras	Morocco	Seychelles	Zimbabwe
China, Macao SAR	India	Mozambique	Sierra Leone	
Colombia	Indonesia	Myanmar	Singapore	
Comoros				

Source: World Health Organization Global Health Observatory, Tuberculosis Incidence 2014. Countries and territories with incidence rates of ≥ 20 cases per 100,000 population. For future updates, refer to http://www.who.int/tb/country/en/.

Have you had frequent or prolonged visits* to one or more of the countries or territories listed above with a high prevalence of TB disease? (If yes, CHECK the countries or territories, above)   ☐ Yes   ☐ No

Have you been a resident and/or employee of high-risk congregate settings (e.g., correctional facilities, long-term care facilities, and homeless shelters)?   ☐ Yes   ☐ No

Have you been a volunteer or health care worker who served clients who are at increased risk for active TB disease?   ☐ Yes   ☐ No

Have you ever been a member of any of the following groups that may have an increased incidence of latent *M. tuberculosis* infection or active TB disease: medically underserved, low-income, or abusing drugs or alcohol?   ☐ Yes   ☐ No

If the answer is YES to any of the above questions, [insert your college/university name] requires that you receive TB testing as soon as possible but at least prior to the start of the subsequent semester).

If the answer to all of the above questions is NO, no further testing or further action is required.

* *The significance of the travel exposure should be discussed with a health care provider and evaluated.*

---

[1]The American College Health Association has published guidelines on "Tuberculosis Screening and Targeted Testing of College and University Students." To obtain the guidelines, visit http://www.acha.org/Guidelines.

(continued)

SAMPLE IMMUNIZATION RECORD (CONTD.)

TUBERCULOSIS (TB) RISK ASSESSMENT (to be completed by **health care provider**)

Clinicians should review and verify the information above. Persons answering YES to any of the questions in Part M are candidates for either Mantoux tuberculin skin test (TST) or Interferon Gamma Release Assay (IGRA), unless a previous positive test has been documented.

History of a positive TB skin test or IGRA blood test? (If yes, document below)   Yes _____ No _____

History of BCG vaccination? (If yes, consider IGRA if possible.)   Yes _____ No _____

1. TB Symptom Check

Does the student have signs or symptoms of active pulmonary tuberculosis disease?   Yes _____ No _____   *If No, proceed to 2 or 3*

If yes, check below:

- ❑ Cough (especially if lasting for 3 weeks or longer) with or without sputum production
- ❑ Coughing up blood (hemoptysis)
- ❑ Chest pain
- ❑ Loss of appetite
- ❑ Unexplained weight loss
- ❑ Night sweats
- ❑ Fever

Proceed with additional evaluation to exclude active tuberculosis disease including tuberculin skin testing, chest x-ray, and sputum evaluation as indicated.

2. Tuberculin Skin Test (TST)

(TST result should be recorded as actual millimeters (mm) of induration, transverse diameter; if no induration, write "0". The TST interpretation should be based on mm of induration as well as risk factors.)**

Date Given: ___/___/___   Date Read: ___/___/___
          M D Y   M D Y

Result: _______ mm of induration   **Interpretation: positive____ negative____

Date Given: ___/___/___   Date Read: ___/___/___
          M D Y   M D Y

Result: _______ mm of induration   **Interpretation: positive____ negative____

**Interpretation guidelines

>5 mm is positive:
- Recent close contacts of an individual with infectious TB
- persons with fibrotic changes on a prior chest x-ray, consistent with past TB disease
- organ transplant recipients and other immunosuppressed persons (including receiving equivalent of >15 mg/d of prednisone for >1 month.)
- HIV-infected persons

>10 mm is positive:
- recent arrivals to the U.S. (<5 years) from high prevalence areas or who resided in one for a significant* amount of time
- injection drug users
- mycobacteriology laboratory personnel
- residents, employees, or volunteers in high-risk congregate settings
- persons with medical conditions that increase the risk of progression to TB disease including silicosis, diabetes mellitus, chronic renal failure, certain types of cancer (leukemias and lymphomas, cancers of the head, neck, or lung), gastrectomy or jejunoileal bypass and weight loss of at least 10% below ideal body weight.

>15 mm is positive:
- persons with no known risk factors for TB who, except for certain testing programs required by law or regulation, would otherwise not be tested.

** The significance of the travel exposure should be discussed with a health care provider and evaluated.*

3. Interferon Gamma Release Assay (IGRA)

Date Obtained: ___/___/___   (specify method) QFT-GIT T-Spot other_____
               M D Y

Result: negative___   positive___   indeterminate___   borderline___ (T-Spot only)

Date Obtained: ___/___/___   (specify method) QFT-GIT T-Spot other_____
               M D Y

Result: negative___   positive___   indeterminate___   borderline___ (T-Spot only)

(continues)

SAMPLE IMMUNIZATION RECORD (CONTD.)

4. Chest x-ray: (Required if TST or IGRA is positive)

Date of chest x-ray: ___/___/___   Result: normal____ abnormal_____
                  M   D   Y

Management of Positive TST or IGRA

All students with a positive TST or IGRA with no signs of active disease on chest x-ray should receive a recommendation to be treated for latent TB with appropriate medication. However, students in the following groups are at increased risk of progression from LTBI to TB disease and should be prioritized to begin treatment as soon as possible.

- Infected with HIV
- Recently infected with *M. tuberculosis* (within the past 2 years)
- History of untreated or inadequately treated TB disease, including persons with fibrotic changes on chest radiograph consistent with prior TB disease
- Receiving immunosuppressive therapy such as tumor necrosis factor-alpha (TNF) antagonists, systemic corticosteroids equivalent to/greater than 15 mg of prednisone per day, or immunosuppressive drug therapy following organ transplantation
- Diagnosed with silicosis, diabetes mellitus, chronic renal failure, leukemia, or cancer of the head, neck, or lung
- Have had a gastrectomy or jejunoileal bypass
- Weigh less than 90% of their ideal body weight
- Cigarette smokers and persons who abuse drugs and/or alcohol

**Populations defined locally as having an increased incidence of disease due to *M. tuberculosis*, including medically underserved, low-income populations

________Student agrees to receive treatment

________Student declines treatment at this time

____

HEALTH CARE PROVIDER

Name ____   Signature ____

Address ______________________________________   Phone (________)________________________________

____

END of SAMPLE FORM
If reproduced for use by a college or university health center, please insert your health center's contact information.
This form should not be returned to ACHA.

Prepared by ACHA's Vaccine-Preventable Diseases Advisory Committee

Revised April 2016

1362 Mellon Road, Suite 180   Hanover, MD 21076 | (410) 859-1500   www.acha.org

Study

- Desk
- Office Chair
- Desk Accessories
- Desk/Floor Lamp
- Bookcase
- Docking Station
- Book Light
- Light Bulbs
- Bulletin Board
- Dry-Erase Board
- Waste Basket
- Paper Shredder
- Laptop
- Web Cam
- Speakers
- Lap Desk
- Wireless Mouse
- Wireless Keyboard
- USB Drive
- Printer
- Ink Cartridges
- Printer Paper
- Surge Protector
- Extension Cord
- Cables/HDMI
- Portable Hard Driver
- Notebooks
- College-Ruled Paper
- Pencils/Pens
- Calculator

Relax

- TV
- TV Stand
- DVD Player
- Futon
- Lounge Chair
- Ottoman
- Floor Cushion
- Toss Pillow
- Floor Lamp
- Backrest
- Throw
- Area Rug
- Window Panels
- Picture Frames
- Candles
- Wall Art
- Digital Music Player
- Headphones/Speakers
- Wall Clock
- Video Game System
- E-Book Reader
- Tablet Computer
- Batteries
- Oscillating Fan
- Bean Bag Chair
- Air Fresheners
- Door Mirror
- Live Plant
- Duct Tape
- Air Purifier

Sleep

- Comforter
- Sheet Set
- Blanket
- Bed Skirt
- Bedding Set
- Bed Pillows
- Pillow Protector
- Body Pillow
- Mattress Pad
- Foam Mattress Topper
- Bedside Table
- Bedside Caddy
- Alarm Clock/Radio
- Mood Fountain
- Pajamas/Sleep Pants
- Window Curtains
- Curtain Rod

Eat

- Mini Refrigerator
- Coffee Maker
- Skillet & Saucepan
- Plates & Bowls
- Glasses & Cups
- Flatware
- Utensils
- Knife/Spoon/Fork
- Cutting Board
- Mixing Bowls
- Microwave
- Microwave Cart
- TV Trays
- Toaster Oven
- Mini Grill
- Can/Bottle Opener
- Food Containers
- Food Storage Bags
- Paper Plates
- Shelf Liner
- Ice Cube Trays
- Bar Stool
- Kettle
- Dish Soap/Rags
- Garbage Bags
- Water Bottle
- Plastic Cups
- Plastic Cutlery
- Mac & Cheese
- Popcorn
- Noodle Soup
- Peanut Butter
- Coffee
- Cereal
- Vitamins
- Snack Food
- Drinks

Shower

- Towels
- Wash Cloths
- Bath Rug
- Tub Mat
- Shower Curtain/Liner
- Curtain Rings
- Robe
- Flip Flops
- Soap Holder
- Shower Caddy
- Shower Radio
- Vanity Mirror
- Toothbrush
- Toothpaste
- Mouthwash/Rinse
- Shampoo
- Conditioner
- Blow Dryer
- Facial Cleanser
- Body Wash/Bar Soap
- Razors
- Lotion
- Shave Gel
- Deodorant
- Beauty Products
- Body Spray
- Hair Styling Products
- Loofah
- Band Aids
- Facial Tissues

Organize

- Storage Tote
- Under Bed Storage
- Shoe Storage
- Garment Storage
- Bed Risers / Lifts
- Closet Organizer
- Wall Shelves
- Drawer Organizers
- Space Bags
- Hangers
- Command Hooks
- Iron/Ironing Board
- Sewing Kit
- Scissors/Tape
- Pop Up Hamper
- Step Stool
- Laundry Basket
- Valuables Safe
- Batteries
- First Aid Kit
- Luggage
- Vacuum
- Drying Rack
- Laundry Detergent
- Tool Set
- Paper Towel
- Broom/Dust Pan
- Disinfecting Wipes
- Sponges
- Mop/Bucket

PERSONALITY PROFILE

How Do You Describe Yourself?

Circle the qualities that you have. Underline the qualities that you would like to work on.

Talented	Accurate	Thoughtful	Athletic
Artistic	Ask Questions	Funny	Bold
Cautious	Daring	Descriptive	Ready
Efficient	Excited	Calm	Confident
Creative	Get It Done	Courteous	Dedicated
Dependable	Privileged	Happy	Hopeful
Handy	Skillful	Knowledgeable	Nervous
Independent	Kind	Social	Hard Worker
On time	Generous	Patient	Stressed
Team player	Motivated	Driven	Relaxed
Comfortable	Innovative	Positive	Honest
Anchoes	Energetic	Flavorful	Tired
Friendly	Spicy	Messy	Tidy
Cheery	Moody	Amazing	Helpful

More about You

Visualize your future, then write what possibilities could be.
Short-term Goals
1.
2.
Midterm Goals
1.
2.
Long-term Goals
1.
2.

ABOUT THE AUTHOR

A.J. Sherman is a wife and a mom of 20 years. However, she is no stranger when it comes to "education and teaching". She was a valedictorian in the Baltimore City Public School System. One of her many accomplishments to date is: An Associates of Arts Degree- (A.A.) and a Bachelors Of Science Degree-(B.S.). She enjoys reading, cooking, having fun and shopping. Also, helping people and donating to the local charities in her community; Baltimore, Maryland where she lives. It is a must that she shares motivational insight about the colleges and the importance of hard work. A.J. Sherman is blessed in her everyday endeavors while going through life's trials and tribulations.